My Mother's Charms

MY MOTHER'S CHARMS

Timeless Gifts of Family Wisdom

Kathleen Oldford

HarperSanFrancisco
A Division of HarperCollinsPublishers

My Mother's Charms: *Timeless Gifts of Family Wisdom*. Copyright © 2002 by Kathleen Oldford. All rights reserved. Printed in Singapore. No part of this book may be used or reproduced in any manner whatsoever without written permission except in the case of brief quotations embodied in critical articles and reviews. For information address HarperCollins Publishers, Inc., 10 East 53rd Street, New York, NY 10022.

HarperCollins books may be purchased for educational, business, or sales promotional use. For information please write: Special Markets Department, HarperCollins Publishers, Inc., 10 East 53rd Street, New York, NY 10022.

HarperCollins Web site: http://www.harpercollins.com

HarperCollins™, 👑 ®, and HarperSanFrancisco™ are trademarks of HarperCollins Publishers, Inc.

FIRST EDITION

DESIGN: Esther Mitgang, BookWorks San Francisco

Library of Congress Cataloging-in-Publication Data
Oldford, Kathleen
  My mother's charms / Kathleen Oldford.—1st ed.
    p. cm.
  Includes biography references.
  ISBN 0-06-251762-7 (cloth : alk. paper)
  1. Family. 2. Bracelets. 3. Oldford, Kathleen—Biography. I. Title.
  HQ734. O583 2001
    306.85—dc21   2001024696
01 02 03 04 05 06 IMA 10 9 8 7 6 5 4 3 2 1

This book is lovingly dedicated to the mothers in my family; departed, living, and yet to be.

⤙ •• ⤚

ACKNOWLEDGMENTS

I've been blessed with the best supporting cast an author could hope for in the birth of her first book.

I'd like to thank my agent, Rita Rozenkranz; my editor, Renee Sedliar; and my designer, Esther Mitgang, for their instincts, insights, and hard work in transforming my words and pictures into such a beautiful book. Indescribable thanks to my parents, Bob and Pat Oldford, for giving me the precious gift of their stories. And finally, I am speechless with thanks to my husband, Mark Sydow, for his patience, tenacity, and late nights spent teaching me the secrets of Adobe Photoshop.

CONTENTS

The sound of my mother's charm bracelet jingling on her wrist always told me she was going someplace special—a party, a wedding, maybe a play. Before she would leave, she'd hold out her wrist and let my sister and me play with the charms of our choice. We always played with the ones that moved. We opened the lid on the candy box, turned the wheel on the windmill, popped out the dog from the doghouse, or wiggled the jointed fish. My mother would make a last-minute check to see that we were snug in our jammies with a bowl of popcorn between us, still warm from the stove. Then she would give final instructions to the baby-sitter and disappear in a cloud of Joy perfume and fur. Even now I can hear the fading sound of her bracelet as she clacked down the hallway off to what I imagined to be the queen's castle.

In 1999 I inherited this bracelet from my mother, along with two others from my grandmother, who passed away in 1992.

These three bracelets joined the other two I had created through my own collecting. As I looked at the five bracelets, I was overcome by how much of my life was staring back at me from these eighty or ninety charms. I saw the little gold bathtub and remembered when my grandmother Elsie would go on safari in Africa. Staring at the thimble charm, I heard my mother's lessons on the importance of stewardship. Looking at Santa popping out of the little gold boot, I felt the excitement of lying awake with my sister Christmas morning waiting for the sun to rise. I wondered if family jewelry had the same effect on other people. Are the stories and emotions of other men and women tightly bound up in the earrings, necklaces, and bracelets worn by the women in their families? Indeed, some casual research revealed that I am not alone in my emotional attachment to family jewelry. A close friend of mine told me that she couldn't look at a string of pearls without thinking about the baking she used to do as a little girl in her Aunt Sansy's kitchen in Charlotte, North Carolina. A fifty-year-old man I met on a plane headed for

Palm Beach described a blue diamond brooch he remembered his grandmother wearing when she read chapters from her favorite mystery novels to him before bedtime. A parking attendant told me all about her mother's struggle to raise six children after I commented on a ring I noticed she was wearing when she handed me my change. Everyone, it seems, has a favorite story about jewelry.

My Mother's Charms features anecdotes that surround four women, each represented by one of four bracelets. The stories in "Elsie's Bracelet" (my grandmother), "Pat's Bracelet" (my mother), and "Anne's Bracelet" (my sister) are based on events in our family history as I remember them. I confess some embellishment here and there, but it comes only through a child's eyes, as I kept my adult self at bay, where she belongs.

The fourth bracelet, Aunt Maxine's, is a color wheel of many other women who have influenced me, including friends, mothers of friends, and quirky acquaintances. It is the love and wisdom of these many wonderful women in my life that I've sought to share.

ELSIE'S

BRACELET

RAF FIGHTER PLANE

ELSIE – JIM'S PLANE SHOT DOWN OVER GERMANY STOP NO SURVIVORS STOP MEMORIAL TUESDAY NEXT STOP *(telegram from Elsie's father, Pop, September 29, 1944)*

At 33, Elsie's brother Jim was one of the most experienced and daring pilots of Britain's Royal Air Force during the years of the Second World War. Like a movie matinee idol he came back from missions again and again without a scratch. His safety seemed forever assured. So, when his plane was shot down, Elsie retreated into a powerful grief, angrily pushing friends, family, and the world far away. Almost a year after Jim's death, she stopped to look in a jewelry store window and spied a little gold plane charm with a tiny RAF insignia on each wing. She bought it on the spot, and as the jeweler was wrapping it up for her, he made a casual comment that changed her life. "They say it's not the takeoff that counts," he said, "it's how well you land the plane." At that moment Elsie realized that the one terrible day of Jim's death could never overshadow all the wonderful years of his life. Over the next few months, it was the fond memories of her brother that would act as beacons to lead her out of her stormy grief and land her safely back to life.

12

Elsie's Bracelet

WEDDING RING

In her twenty-first year, Elsie was determined to marry Tom O'Keefe, a young newspaper reporter from Long Island.

Though handsome and full of ambition, Tom was not from the fine society family Pop had envisioned for his daughter. But, like the fathers of countless independent, headstrong daughters, he was defeated in any attempt to prevent the match.

It was the birth of his granddaughter, Patricia, in 1930 that finally brought Pop around. One day Pop sat next to Elsie holding little Patricia. Looking down at his granddaughter, Pop gave the baby her first piece of advice: "Remember, little one, God makes the match. The rest of us are only here to *help* him in his work, not to get in the way of it."

Elsie's Bracelet

In 1941, ten years after the death of her first husband, Elsie met and fell in love with a vivacious, kind man named Hagy. Twelve months later, war called Hagy to its battle lines. He pledged his love to Elsie with a parting gift of a new charm for her bracelet—a tiny gold letter with her initials, EFO, on the address side and his initials, RWH, engraved on the back. Separated by Hitler's madness, they wrote to each other every day for two years, sometimes twice a day. To Elsie, the little gold letter charm on her bracelet was the promise that Hagy would return soon and safely. Without the pressure of conversation, they expressed deep personal feelings with an honesty and passion that surprised them both. But it was through this intense correspondence that Elsie and Hagy realized that marriage between them was not to be. Elsie never discussed their decision with anyone. Her last letter was very difficult to write, but it was for the best. Hagy's reply would inspire her to remain a prolific letter writer throughout her long life. In the midst of sadness he wrote, "Elsie, you have always known how I value the writing and receipt of letters. It's the best way for me to talk when I can't speak the words, and it's the only way I can listen when my heart is hard of hearing."

Elsie's Bracelet

HAND MIXER

Elsie couldn't roast a walnut or boil water, but she could bake Betty Crocker right out of the kitchen. Even her batter was delicious. My sister and I would perch on our chairs like little birds waiting for a spoon or beater loaded with the gooey, sweet paste of that morning's surprise. But no one in the family could ever get a real recipe out of Elsie. Sure, she'd list all the basic ingredients, along with helpful hints about beating, folding, and rolling. But even when her instructions were followed to the letter, the end result never tasted quite the same. With her hand on the family Bible, Elsie swore she never left a thing out when she shared her recipes. Even her sister, Kay, couldn't pry any missing details out of her. Shortly before she died, Elsie sent me her handpainted recipe box. Each recipe was typed neatly on a single three-by-five card and wrapped in cellophane. Something else in the box caught my attention. Taped to the inside of the top was a folded piece of paper. Reading it, I smiled a teary smile. There was the secret ingredient to every cookie and pie she ever took out of the oven: *Dear Kathleen, Remember, it's not the cake you bake that makes you great. It's the love you add when beating the batter that matters.*

Elsie's Bracelet

When I was nine years old I asked Elsie why she had a little Dutch shoe on her bracelet. She said, "Everyone knows I *always* go Dutch treat. It's what all well-bred ladies do." Not wanting to seem like a moron about something that my grandmother clearly thought was important, I called my best friend, Janice, the undisputed source of all things hip, and asked her to fill me in. "Oh, that's easy," she said. "That's when women get together and dance slow dances with each other wearing old shoeboxes on their feet that they decorate to look like the wooden shoes everyone wore in that movie called *The Silver Skates*." I took her word for it. Soon after, my mother told me to get ready because Elsie was taking us out "Dutch treat." I came clomping down the stairs in my "wooden shoes" held on by rubber bands, wearing my pink party dress. Mother's and Elsie's mouths dropped open. I explained what Janice had said. Then Elsie took me back up to my room and helped me change into my Mary Janes. Bending to buckle my shoe, she said, "You'll save yourself a lot of time and trouble if you remember that anyone can know the right question to ask, but only smart people know to ask the right person."

WINDMILL

Barry Baretta, Elsie's second husband, gave her the windmill charm during a trip to Holland in 1962. He chose this charm over the rest because he could spin the little sail wheel. It was a sail wheel, he told her, that had once given him hope when hope was hard to find. In July 1940, depression-racked Holland was reeling from the German occupation. Over just a few months, panic and fear had forced honest men in the city to commit desperate acts. But Barry, then married to his first wife, vowed he would not surrender to that terror. Steadfastly, he held on to daily routines to keep his family reassured and his mind above the chaos in the streets. Every day near dusk Barry gathered his wife and two young sons by the window to sing a song to the old windmill up the hill. To Barry, the methodical turning was the reassuring beat of every Dutchman's heart—strong, continuous, and unstoppable. It was this heart that would save beloved Holland. In a whisper, they sang to the windmill each day: "Round and round and round you go, never sleeping, never slow. In the worst of winds we know, always, always round you'll go."

Elsie's Bracelet

WISHBONE

Every other Sunday my mother would cook a turkey. The wishbone was set aside and put up in the cupboard to dry. After a few days, Elsie and I would break it and make a wish. I always wished for a pony—a golden palomino just like the one Roy Rogers rode. I was going to call him Goldy, and he was going to live in the garage. I'd wrap my tiny pinkie finger around my half of the bone as carefully as a baseball player securing his grip around the bat. Elsie would do the same, always trying to counterbalance my grip to tip the odds in my favor. We'd close our eyes, squeeze our pinkies tight, count to three, and pull. At the snap of the bone my eyes would fly open. Tears would always appear if I ended up with the short piece of the bone, my wish never to be. Taking me into her arms she'd whisper, "Don't worry, Kathleen. I wished for your wish. And as long as you keep wishing, I'll keep wishing too."

Elsie's Bracelet

Every Sunday my family went to a little white clapboard church with hard mahogany pews and scarlet kneelers. The rector there was known for his sermons concerning the "intellectual interpretation of the many implications of sin."

After I'd been exposed to his perspective countless Sundays, my childhood impression of God was that he was a pretty impatient guy who loved rule books and scorecards. Fortunately for me, God explained his true nature by speaking to me through a poem Elsie wrote. She shared it with me one day during a weepy phone call. The poem was a beautiful song about the complex nature of God's desire to have a love relationship with each of us. One verse caught my attention and continues to encourage me. Of our Creator she wrote, "God doesn't want indentured souls; he seeks a lover's heart."

Diamonds may be some girls' best friends, but pearls were Elsie's bosom buddies. Her favorite necklace was a choker strung with pearls the size of gum balls. When I was eight years old, the only other woman I knew who wore pearls that size was Wilma Flintstone. This concerned me at the time, so I asked Elsie if she would please wear smaller pearls that didn't look so funny. Standing with me in front of the mirror she said, "I love wearing these pearls just because they're so big and different. They're just like some of the people I meet. Some of them may be a little strange and out of place, but the very thing that makes them strange is what makes them beautiful too."

Elsie had me playing gin rummy with her when I still needed a phone book tucked under my behind to see across the table. Both of my small hands could barely hold my ten cards, so she would have to pick up and discard for me. Between games she'd use the face cards in the deck to tell detailed stories about my great-aunts and great-uncles and my great-great-grand-mother Nana and her husband, Pop. One of her favorite cards was her brother, my great-uncle Jim. He usually turned up as the jack of spades. Trouble seemed to track him like a bloodhound. He regularly found himself in the

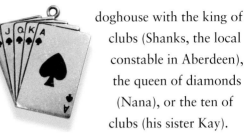

doghouse with the king of clubs (Shanks, the local constable in Aberdeen), the queen of diamonds (Nana), or the ten of clubs (his sister Kay).

The exact nature of his various indiscretions was never explained, but they seemed to merit pretty stiff punishment, not unlike the kind I encountered when I stuffed all my clothes under the bed to clean my room. It was comforting to me that my great-uncle seemed to get in as much trouble as I did. I can still see her holding up the jack of spades and the jack of diamonds, telling me, "Kathleen, it seems to me that you and Jim make a great pair."

Elsie was a champion bridge player who insisted that rules be followed to the letter. All the members of her bridge club considered Elsie's word final, and she was routinely asked to settle disputes at other tables. When it came to family play she was just as serious. Hand after hand, she would correct our bridge etiquette and advise our play, citing rules and standards. During one family game, my mother called Elsie on an improper play. Indignant, Elsie recited the rule in her defense with the impatience of a teacher explaining to a three-year-old that no, cows don't live in refrigerators.

Mother persisted. My father finally looked in the rule book and pointed out that Elsie was wrong. Elsie was astounded that she was being challenged. Throwing down her cards, she spat, "The hell with the rules!" She got up, knocking down her folding chair as she rose, and huffed off to the living room. Minutes later she returned, chuckling at herself. In later years, when the story was retold, Elsie reminded us that if she had learned only one thing in life, it was that "Anger is just comedy that takes itself too seriously."

NUT AND BOLT

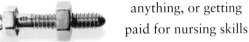

My great-aunt, Kay, gave Elsie this charm, a gift from the hardware company my great-uncle worked for in the thirties. It turned out to be representative of Elsie's work ethic. She always told me that work, which consumes most of the fleeting hours in this life, has hundreds of definitions. Work may be learning how to bowl, volunteering at the soup kitchen, fixing the leaky pipe in the bathroom, getting your teenager to do anything, or getting paid for nursing skills practiced during the night shift at the hospital. The energy and time this lifework demands should move you to choose each commitment carefully. Elsie believed that once your choice of work was made, you should work hard every day with relish and joy, never wasting a moment. She said I'd find that when I gave my best, the best would come.

FAN

Bette worked with Elsie as a typist in the Chrysler Building in NYC one summer during World War II. Most offices were without air conditioning, so the thirty-sixth floor was hot as an oven. Bette always looked fresh and cool regardless of the time of day. Elsie, on the other hand, would be pushing hair out of her makeup-smeared face, fanning herself with a folder to keep from fainting, and wishing she had some way of changing out of her dress, which was always wrinkled and damp by ten in the morning. Then one day Elsie got her first lesson in creative problem solving on the job. She walked into the ladies' room at break time and saw a cord snaking from the outlet on the floor and disappearing under the wall of the end stall. A ping-ping-ping whirring sound came from behind the stall door. She knocked on the door, and it opened to reveal Bette standing on the toilet with her hands braced against the opposite wall and an electric fan lying on the floor face up to blow air under her dress. "Honey," she said, "there's nothing like a little wind up the old drawers to freshen a girl up!"

CANDY BOX

To Elsie, eating domestic chocolate was like eating cardboard dusted with cocoa powder. For her the only *real* chocolate in the world came from Switzerland, preferably the two-pound double-layered assortment box from Lindt. Elsie said that a box of Lindt chocolates covered all the major food groups. But Elsie had an annoying habit of picking a chocolate out of the box and taking a little nip to discern the flavor. If she didn't care for it she'd place it back in its paper candy cup and move on to the next piece. After a couple of days we were left with a box of little chocolate accident victims that had sustained varying degrees of trauma, including two or three we couldn't save. Members of the family got so fed up with her that we ended up always buying two boxes of the same chocolate—one for Elsie and one for everyone else. Elsie never understood why her taste tests bothered other people. It made perfect sense to her to take appropriate measures to avoid unpleasant experiences. Without apology she would tell us, "Behind every temptation lurks the risk of a bad taste. I say always try a bit before you commit."

SPITTOON

Elsie was a self-admitted celebrity gossip. Years before the tabloids blasted their headlines from the racks at supermarket checkouts, Elsie knew what was what in Hollywood. Affairs, marriages, divorces, illegitimate children, and behavior on the set—she could rattle off the juicy details on most of the big stars of the 1960s. She could even name Elizabeth Taylor's four favorite colors of nail polish.

But when it came to her friends and neighbors, the less they told her the better. She simply didn't want to hear their *As the World Turns* moments over coffee. Conversations about secret spousal habits, coupon clipping, and any developmental updates concerning a person under five were especially unwelcome. She wanted to be sure that we would never exhibit such bad behavior. Her favorite admonishment to us on the subject was,

"Telling people about private matters is like spitting in public. It's a nasty habit that leaves behind something of yours that people would rather not see."

Elsie's Bracelet

Elsie came to stay with us one time when my parents vacationed in Florida. Before she left, my mother gave us strict instructions: my brother was to cut the lawn, and my sister had to clean the bathroom. I was charged with the one chore I hated most—dusting the furniture. I launched into feverish bargaining mode and tried to reach another settlement, but by the time my mother left for Palm Beach I was still the designated duster. A few days later I heard the three words I was dreading come floating cheerily out from the kitchen: "Time to dust, Kathleen." Twenty minutes later, she stomped out to get me. Dropping the can of Pledge and a cloth in my lap, she explained that certain jobs in this life had to get done and I'd have to do them whether I felt like it or not. Then she looked at me to be sure I was listening. "Kathleen," she said, "a dog doesn't stop wanting to eat just because you don't feel like feeding it!" It wasn't the last time Elsie had to remind me of my responsibilities. After I got married and dillydallied on some thank-you notes, she pointed to her little doghouse charm and said, "You better feed that dog." Okay, where's the can opener?

Elsie's Bracelet

"I LOVE YOU" SPINNER

Elsie called this her "motion picture charm." The letters I, L, V, Y, U appear on one side of a little spinner, and the letters O, E, O on the other. When you spin the spinner you see the full phrase "I LOVE YOU." To Elsie, this charm was a perfect symbol for the unit of a couple. Each half of the couple has a set of letters—abilities, resources, expectations, even DNA—different from the other half. A love match happens when we meet someone who has the right set of corresponding letters. "But be careful," she used to warn us. "It doesn't matter how much you think you love someone; if his letters don't work with your letters, the only thing you'll ever spell is disaster."

Elsie's Bracelet

BATHTUB

We all knew that Elsie loved her baths. She and Barry spent weeks on African safari each year, and Elsie always made time for her favorite ritual. Between baths she'd venture out with cameras to capture the raw, unspoiled beauty of the Serengeti Plain in the 1960s. Combining those photographs with her letters, we pieced together a rich narrative of a life at camp that offered few luxuries, many hardships, and astounding sights. But a daily bath was one thing Elsie would not leave behind. While the Nigerian guides considered this requirement for a bath more than a little strange, they were happy to accommodate their favorite client. "Oh, I'm sure they all think I'm daft about this bath business," she wrote in one letter to my mother, "but they accommodate me. It's worth all the bother, though. It's the only place in the world where I can sit in a warm tub of water, wearing just my bath cap, and watch zebra and elephants meander by just yards away. Extraordinary adventures are often hidden in life's most basic tasks."

29

Elsie's Bracelet

PAT'S

BRACELET

BABY CARRIAGE

My mother put a lot of miles on the family baby carriage. She pushed the three of us on journeys and jaunts from the moment we came home from the hospital. The carriage gave us our first glimpses of life outside the nursery while keeping us safe from wind, sun, and showers. Throughout our lives, my mother worked to shield us from the rawness of life. She believed it was her job to give us happy, lasting memories of our childhood to comfort us in times of trouble in our adult lives. After we were out in the world, each of us inevitably wandered home from time to time, discouraged over the messiness of life. My mother always made us feel better by getting us to laugh over some funny event from our childhood. "Remember that God gives you the gift of memory to serve as your helper," she said, "and he gives you a childhood because he knows that's where all of the best helpers come from."

OUTHOUSE

My mother always taught us to gauge our progress in life against our previous circumstances, not the current circumstances of others. My mother learned this from her own mother, Elsie. As young girls in the 1920s, Elsie and her sister, Kay, spent summers at the beach, where the family went to escape the brutal heat of New York City. They would stay in a rustic, rented cottage, a different one each year. Upon arrival, both girls would race around the house and the property, tallying up all of the new rental's pluses and minuses. One summer the girls found themselves in a cottage next to a huge beachfront estate with gardens, servants, a tennis court, and a tree house. While some children might have moped around and been envious of the children next door, Elsie and Kay saw their situation a little differently. Elsie ran up to Kay, breathless with excitement. "Kay, Kay, come on and see the outhouse. We've got a two-holer this year!"

THIMBLE

My mother gave the gift of a charitable heart to each of her children. Together we would renovate our old toys so we could give them to others who were less fortunate. When we tired of a toy, we carefully put it aside in the charity box. There it would wait until the end of the year. Then my mother would pull out her needle, thread, and thimble to fix a torn ear on a stuffed bear or hem a doll's drooping skirt. My father would reattach handles and paint scraped wheels. Our job was to sort the girls' toys from the boys' and box them accordingly. Then we all proudly took the boxes down to the Goodwill store. Most of the toys looked like they'd just come out of the box. As my mother sewed and scissored she reminded us that "no off-the-shelf gift can ever compare with a from-the-heart labor of love."

GOAT

One of my favorite childhood games was "If You Were an Animal." Our mother used the game to help my brother, Neal,  and me understand each other so we wouldn't quarrel over our differences. The game involved taking turns describing each other as an animal. The description could be made up of the personality traits, physical characteristics, or habits of any mammal, fish, bird, or insect. I remember telling my brother he was a bear. He growled at me a lot, but he wasn't really mean. I learned that my brother saw me as lion—strong and always ready to attack—so I tried to be more patient with him. The game was so easy to understand that even our little sister, Anne, gleefully participated, throwing inanimate objects into the mix. House, pencil, hot dog, and car were some of her favorites. But one day she helped us appreciate the creature common to all of our lives when she took a turn with my mother and said, "Mommy, if you were an animal you'd be a mommy one."

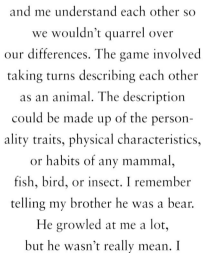

ICE TONGS

In January 1952 my parents announced their engagement and, as was customary, my mother and Elsie were invited for a weekend stay with my father's family. The first thing my mother noticed when she walked in the door of the New England cottage was that everyone was wearing multiple layers of clothing. It seemed that a cozy visit of cocoa and roaring fires was not in the offing. My mother and Elsie were shown upstairs where they made an unsettling discovery: the second floor had no heat. Each night they huddled like stranded explorers at the North Pole praying for daylight. In the morning, whimpering, they leaped from bed to clothes the moment breakfast was called. Concerned about the extreme nature of my father's circumstances, my mother came close to calling off the engagement. Fortunately for me, her heart put things in perspective and she married my father on a balmy September afternoon. She credits the warmth of my father's attention throughout her freezing stay for reassuring her that she had made the right choice. "From that day forward I knew," she once told me, "ice would never form around the well-tended fire of our committed hearts."

GOLF CLUBS

My mother is a gracious golfer. She takes her bad days on the course the same as she takes her good days—all in stride, and with a smile. When she plays with someone just learning the game, she goes out of her way to offer encouragement. When asked, she never hesitates to suggest tips for better play. She believes talent is a gift to share with others, not a prize to be hoarded. This charm, given to her by my father, symbolizes her helper's heart and reminds me that helping others along the way is the wise and compassionate choice.

Pat's Bracelet

OWL

I met my first owl while reading *Winnie-the-Pooh*. One day my mother suggested that while Owl was a wise creature, he was a bit of a know-it-all. When I asked her what the word meant, she pointed to chapter 8: "And Owl was telling Kanga an Interesting Anecdote full of long words like *Encyclopedia* . . ." She explained, "See how Owl likes to use big words when little ones would do? He's trying to show Kanga how smart he is. "Maybe," she went on, "Owl would be better off using words that were easier for Kanga to understand. And then Kanga might not be so cross with him. "Before I open my mouth now, I hear a whisper from the Hundred Acre Woods, "Trying to be smart may not always be the wise thing to do."

Pat's Bracelet

CAN OPENER

When my sister, Anne, was four, she wanted to know what a can of worms was. Anne watched plenty of *Sesame Street*, so she could easily identify a worm (the letter W). And she ate plenty of canned tomato soup, so she knew what a can was. But the combination of the two baffled her, and my mother's explanation didn't help. From the child's seat in the super-market cart she pleaded for my mother to take her to the place in the store where the cans of worms were kept. She begged any adult who wandered in her path for a can of worms to play with.

Realizing that the actual explanation wasn't ever going to be enough, my mother resorted to a toddler's perspective. She took an old dog food can, filled it with dirt from the garden, plopped a few fat, slimy worms on top, and presented it to my sister. When my sister opened the can, she was horrified. She dropped it and ran back to the house screaming, "Fingers! There's fingers in there! Take them away!" Today my mother is careful with the explanations she gives to her grandchildren because she knows a can of fingers when she sees one.

Pat's Bracelet

My mother approaches gardening like a football lineman—she tackles her opponent hard and as many times as possible. Her adversary is anything that keeps her flowers from their task of blooming. She thrusts her hands into a pile of topsoil to bring out any rock or debris that gets in the way of potting her plants. She never cares if she gets sprayed by the hose or steps in horse manure. It doesn't matter how many times she has to replant, weed, soak, and fertilize. Not being a gardener myself, I had a hard time understanding this obsession. But when I started my first job out of college it began to make sense. I was avoiding some tedious research required to finish an important report. My mother urged me to dig into the detail and keep at it until it was done.

Reluctantly, I agreed. Sure, I made a few mistakes here and there, but I got that report done. My mother was right— flowers grow only when I take time to dig in the dirt.

POCKETKNIFE

Okay, I admit it. I joined the Girl Scouts for the clothes. From my perspective, the uniform meant I was an expert. Every month I donned my green outfit, complete with snappy beret, web belt, and cherished sash dotted with merit badges. I was ready, at a moment's notice, to demonstrate my knowledge about all things related to camping. My favorite lecture involved cooking pancakes on an overturned coffee can. Along with the clothes came all sorts of cool gadgets I could buy that were marked with the official Girl Scout insignia. After answering my begging with multiple safety demonstrations, my mother agreed to buy me the pocketknife.

I was now Warrior Girl. On a clandestine mission, I took the pocketknife to school one day to show off my new carving skills to the nonscout girls in my class. Not many hours later, sitting in the enemy camp of the principal, it was clear that my secret agent skills needed work. The knife went back to the store, and I lost my uniform-wearing privileges for a month or two. Before I was allowed to wear my uniform to school again my mother made sure I understood the difference between looking grown up and being grown up. She explained it this way: "A costume may help you look the part, but only experience gives you the privilege to star in the play."

Pat's Bracelet

FISH

Standing out from the crowd is a route to success that's promoted endlessly through television, books, and movies. But my mother pointed to the little fish in the sea, who travels with many other fish out in the deep ocean. In the school of fish he calls home he learns how to avoid predators, find the best food, and locate a mate. The fish may travel to a distant reef by himself from time to time, but by returning to his friends in the school he's able to travel safely and far. The same is true for people. Although each of us is blessed with unique gifts, we need to be willing to pool our resources and talents to solve the larger problems. My mother always encouraged me to look for opportunities to contribute my talents to a group effort. She dangled the fish charm and told me, "Make sure you spend some of your time working with other people. Sometimes you get a lot more accomplished than you would if you were trying to swim out there all by yourself."

Pat's Bracelet

QUEEN'S CARRIAGE

Television in the 1950s featured shows that my mother couldn't get enough of. *Queen for a Day, The Miss America Pageant, This Is Your Life*—my mother loved them all. Like any armchair contestant, she had little patience for the television show guest who won the new Frigidaire only to lose it by saying something stupid at the end of the show. One 1960s Miss America made my mother's point. After being crowned, this contestant gathered her roses and began to walk down the runway, waving to the audience. Tears of joy were streaming down her face as she got to the end of the stage. The camera zoomed in for the final close-up shot. She lifted her gloved hand to her face and proceeded to wipe her runny nose from finger to elbow. My mother was horrified. She used the moment for years after when teaching my sister and me the rules of etiquette. "Remember Miss America," she'd say. "You don't want to win the crown, then lose the kingdom."

DIPLOMA

In 1951 my mother graduated from Boston University with a bachelor of science degree in biology, and her mother gave her this charm. Very few women at that time graduated in the sciences, but my mother had been determined to finish. She wanted to join the battle against cancer and hoped she might contribute one day to its cure. Her zeal was not at all surprising to her classmates and friends, who found her, as she is today, bright, articulate, and always curious about how nature operates.

My mother enrolled in a different kind of educational program five years later at the birth of her first child, my brother, Neal. All of a sudden she found herself with a squealing little bundle who arrived with no instructions. Like other new mothers of every race, education, color, or circumstance, my mother set out on a journey that was part trial and error and part instinct. At times during my brother's childhood, my mother felt like her final exams would never end and her spring break would never come. But today she'll tell you her most cherished degree is her M.M.— Master of Motherhood.

Pat's Bracelet

PICTURE GLOBE

A tiny crinkled photograph of my father's face rests inside this charm. The photo is old and faded and hard to make out. My mother doesn't remember putting the picture inside the charm or even when and where the photo was taken. "It's a bit of a mystery," she says. I will never know all the intricate details of my parents' relationship. I see glimpses of what goes on between them in what they laugh at, what they argue about, or what they like to do together, but the true nature of the chemistry that has kept them together for more than forty years is obscured from my view. And perhaps it's better that way. The depth of the bond between my mother and father, or any longtime partners, can never be fully comprehended. The most we children can see is what the camera shows—a snippet in time, a fragment of the whole. The complete picture eludes us.

EIFFEL TOWER

My parents are travel junkies, so it came as no surprise when they announced their trip to France. I thought how wonderful it would be for them to see the Notre Dame Cathedral, poke around in little antique stores, and eat, eat, eat. Well, that wasn't their plan. They headed off instead to a remote little village in Provence to take a three-week language-immersion course.

These two seventy-year-olds attended class each day with ten other, much younger, aspiring linguists. At night they labored over long hours of homework, reading and writing only in French. Even in their free time they were forced to speak French, because few people in the farming village where they stopped for groceries spoke English. Just buying apples required a lot of thought. My mother later told me that they chose the course because of something that happened during their first trip to France, in 1964.

"We visited the Eiffel Tower and met a shy ninety-three-year-old man there who told us he journeyed to the tower every week. And even though he was afraid of strangers, he made himself talk to at least one foreigner each time he visited. When I asked him why he did this he snorted, 'Madam, it is the very thing that scares you most that you must do if you desire to have a happy, well-lived life.'"

OSTRICH

My mother is a stickler when it comes to pronouncing words. When we were children, the word *ostrich* was at the center of a particularly drawn out skirmish between my father and her. My father's New England accent mangled words without discretion and at a rapid pace. *Car* became "caaaa," *cellar* became "sella," and one day *ostrich* became "aaaaastridge." My mother had had enough. She created a flash card with a picture of an ostrich next to the phonetic spelling of the word. When my father misspoke any word at all, my mother said, "O is for ostrich," and held up the card for my father to see. One day my father was in his chair reading the paper to my mother. Once again, another poorly enunciated word fell out of his mouth. Before my mother could respond, a tiny, exasperated voice rose from behind the chair. "O is for ostrich!" They looked behind the chair to find my three-year-old sister, Anne, hands on hips, glaring up at them. It's not what you say, it's how you phonate.

Pat's Bracelet

SEASHELL

Like the quiet whisper from a seashell, a small, still voice rises from deep inside the heart. "Listen carefully to the voice," the self-improvement pundits say, "and you will learn many things." This may be true. But my mother, in all her wisdom, taught us that this whisper is more than just a voice to listen to; it's a voice we need to answer because the voice is God speaking to us as he seeks us out. He wants to talk with us. Just talk. He's interested in everything going on in our lives, so he's always tapping on our spirit's windowpane with persistence until we answer back. "Talk to that small, still voice," Mother would say. "It's just God checking in to see how you're doing. Tell him how you feel today. Ask for his help on something. Tell him a secret. There's nothing God likes more than a nice, long chat wirh a friend."

TEAPOT

The kettle was put on to boil and taken off just before it whistled. The porcelain Limoges was set out with the tea bag in the cup and the spoon on the saucer. Scalding water was poured into the cup, quickly followed with an ice cube to take the temperature down a few degrees. And the Walkers shortbread was never forgotten. This was how my mother, my grandmother, and my grandmother's sister, Kay, took their tea together. My grandmother and her sister passed away years ago. Without them in the kitchen for company, my mother sits for tea only now and then. But she believes the ritual continues in another place, in another dimension, and that when she sees these two wise women again they will be waiting for her with an extra cup and saucer at the table, the shortbread close at hand. And then the three of them will sit forever, together, sharing secrets and telling stories, drinking from cups that will never run dry.

Pat's Bracelet

ANNE'S

BRACELET

ROLLER SKATE

When Mom asked us to clean out our toy trunk, my sister, Anne, and I would moan and complain. We didn't see the point. We wanted to keep all our toys just in case we needed them later. But we sorted anyway, because we were allowed to keep only as many as would fit in the trunk. When we got older and moved out on our own, we rushed to get grown-up toys. We swapped our roller skates for cars, our Barbie clothes for designer outfits, and our dress-up shows for jobs where we wore grown-up shoes. But by our mid-thirties we realized it was time to clean out the toy trunk once again. Anne made room for the family she wanted to start. I made room for my career goals. Today Mom's whisper to organize our priorities comes more often and at unexpected times. We've gotten a little better at deciding which things to keep and which ones to discard. Without the jumble of possessions long outgrown, we're free to fill the trunk with new pursuits and opportunities. And we're more responsible about the things we add, because at an unexpected time God will call each of us home, and then who needs the clutter?

COWBELL

When we were kids we had our milk delivered to the back door. It came in glass bottles with cardboard lids about the size of a silver dollar. Our milkman drove up our driveway several times a week. We loved to see the huge picture of Elsie the cow smiling at us from the side of the truck. But it was a source of real confusion for Anne that the cow and our grandmother shared the same name. In Anne's three-year-old brain her grandmother Elsie, dressed as a cow, was delivering milk to the back door of every house on our street. Of course Anne was quite proud that her grandmother had such an important job and told her kindergarten class all about it every time cows were discussed. In the end however, several notes from Anne's teacher made it apparent that my mother had to clear things up. Anne finally understood the distinction between Elsie the grandmother and Elsie the cow. Thankfully, her imagination remained innocent. Today she designs and sews dazzling quilts cherished by every person lucky enough to get one. The charm was a gift from Elsie after one of her trips to Switzerland. But for Anne it represents her definition of creative thought. As she says, "A brilliant imagination is simply a collection of wrong impressions left uncorrected."

Anne's Bracelet

POODLE

Anne adored her dog, Frisbee. The dog was the strangest version of a poodle ever born to the breed—long legs like a whippet and a bark like a Siamese cat—but my sister was crazy about her just the same. While Anne was at college, our mother sent news of Frisbee in every letter from home. But while my mother was a faithful letter writer, she hated to deliver bad news. To lessen the blow she would often string two unrelated sentences together, one positive and one negative, hoping that they would equal each other out. "I tried that new brownie cake recipe you sent me," could easily be followed by, "The house burned down last week, but we're all fine." Anne's first experience with this came one day soon after she arrived at school. She was about to fold up a newsy six-pager from my mother when she noticed a teeny-tiny sentence at the bottom. It read, "P.S. Frisbee would have loved the toy you sent, but she died last Tuesday." Though it wasn't funny at the time, Anne now looks back and laughs, "Even the worst news can be lightened by a mother's good intentions."

PLAYING CARDS

When Anne was in college, she had a roommate who urged her to learn bridge. "It's so much fun," she would say, "and you meet such interesting people." Even though Anne had heard the same thing from Elsie when she was growing up, she still had no interest in learning. Frankly, she was a little overwhelmed by the card game. It seemed so complex. Even worse, it appeared she'd have to spend hours playing hand after hand to ever be good at it. After repeated invitations from her friend, she finally gave in. To her surprise, bridge turned out to be pretty simple. Once she learned the rules, it was a lot of fun too. But the hardest skill to master surprised her. It had nothing to do with rule books or bridge etiquette. The real work went into learning how to understand the language of bidding. She told me one day that learning to bid was like working at a relationship. "You're not very good at it in the beginning. But once you've played with your partner for a while you start to understand what he's trying to tell you. As soon as that happens, playing the right card just comes naturally."

TIGER CLAW

In 1961, on one of her many trips to Nairobi, Elsie purchased the tiger claw. At that time there was little emphasis on the health of the environment, so trade in skins, furs, horns, and claws was commonplace. The charm was simply decorative to her, much like the tiger claws worn by the many native people she encountered. After Elsie's death in 1990, Anne inherited the bracelet that had the tiger claw. She struggled over accepting it. On the one hand, the charm was a beautiful piece of jewelry; but on the other, it symbolized the senseless killing of an endangered animal. Uncertain of her feelings, she took the charm off the bracelet and left it with me for quite some time. Anne took back the claw a few years ago. She realized the charm could be a teaching tool. Charm bracelets by their nature spark conversation.

And today, when the claw charm attracts attention, Anne reminds people that sometimes beauty comes at a terrible price, and only humans can protect nature from suffering the cost.

Anne's Bracelet

SOMBRERO

Anne has a natural ease with people. She can make meaningful conversation without preparing for it, and she's expert at bringing a room of strangers together for a discussion at any social gathering. She draws people out through her questions, saying little about herself. When she does talk about herself, it's usually to rescue an awkward situation by telling a personal anecdote. She eases the embarrassment of others by taking it on herself. She says her approach is to work hard at seeing the world through the eyes of people from backgrounds very different from her own. "I like to try on another person's hat so I can see the horizon from a different perspective."

BIBLE

I'd like to say that Anne and I have always been close as sisters, but that's not the case. We were strangers to each other well into our thirties. We disliked each other out of unfamiliarity, inflicting wounds that each of us silently regretted but let stand out of pride. Then one of us stepped toward the other, and the other held out her hand. Once tearful confessions were made and bottled-up longings were released, we found ourselves closer than either of us had thought possible. We don't take any credit for this miracle because we both believe that unseen, loving hands folded us together despite our protests. Today our common religion is sisterhood, and our first and only commandment is unconditional love. We talk on the phone almost every week, commiserate over our little life battles, and, to our astonishment, find we say "I love you" to each other before we part. Once, right before we hung up, my sister paused and said, "You and I are living proof that God pays special attention to the love between sisters. But I think he must have known from the start that sisters need a lot more adult supervision than anyone else."

GLASSES

In her teens, Anne never wore the same pair of sunglasses twice. A few days after a new pair was bought it would disappear to a place she has yet to find. Alien abduction, midnight escapes back to the store, or suicide via the kitchen disposal were the only plausible explanations. We nicknamed her the Queen of Lost Shades. She tried every which way to keep from losing her glasses; she put them on her head, wore them around her neck, put them back on the dresser every night.

At one point she even taped them to her Levis. But no matter what, the glasses always ended up missing in action. Then, finally, she solved her problem. She stopped buying sunglasses. Like discovering a perfect law of physics, she found that once she stopped buying sunglasses, she stopped losing them too. She related her epiphany one day while we were having coffee: "The best strategy is often the last one we'd consider because we're so blinded by our vanity."

GLOBE

I gave Anne the globe because it reminds me of her courage. Her husband is a British engineer in high demand by international corporations with sites in remote locations like the mountains of Peru and the jungles of Southeast Asia. Anne frequently packs up her family and heads off to places unknown to even the most seasoned traveler. To some her life looks like a series of grand adventures, but this type of world travel is hardly glamorous. It's filled with 2:00 A.M. landings at empty air terminals with disoriented toddlers, furniture that arrives months later if at all, and the perils of illness in a town five hours from the nearest hospital. Some women might stay home while their husbands worked abroad. But my sister will do whatever it takes to stay with her husband and keep her children close to their father. If that means putting aside her fear of the unknown, that's what she does. I've always believed that "love makes the world go 'round," but my sister's life has convinced me that it takes courage to keep it spinning steadily on its axis.

PHONOGRAPH

My sister says that songs can do amazing things. You can be riding along in your car, mad at the world, until *wham*, a song begins to play on the radio that suddenly yanks you back to a golden moment. Years melt away, and suddenly you're tossing a Frisbee with your roommates on a warm spring day, eating a hot dog at the family barbecue out back by the pool, or snowbound inside the house watching TV and playing cards with your best friend from next door. All it takes is a few notes or an opening verse of one old, forgotten song.

If you tuck a favorite song away on a tape or CD, it's easy to sing away even the dreariest thoughts. Anne explained the idea one day. "Look at Julie Andrews in *The Sound of Music;* all she did was sing about a few of her favorite things, listen to the Reverend Mother sing about climbing every mountain, and the next thing you know she's got Christopher Plummer wrapped around her little pinkie." Our lives may not work out like the movies, but our memories can come close. Now go turn on your stereo.

CHALET

Many of us are dismayed to find that our possessions are controlling the choices we make. The need to keep acquiring things is so strong in our culture that we find ourselves moving into bigger houses just because we need more storage. Anne lives very differently. After the first few moves, the cost and uncertainty of shipping their things from country to country led my sister and her husband to an eye-opening conclusion: there really was no need to drag around so much stuff. Now every time they move to a new country, they sell or donate anything that requires shipping—furniture, cars, kitchen tools, and appliances, even toys. Once they get to the new destination, they refurnish and replace items according to what's readily available. Today they have the things they need rather than need the things they have. The highest priority on my sister's "living list" is finding a home for her brood. She spends a lot of time assessing the needs of the people in her family, not the stuff the family hauls around from place to place, and then she gets a dwelling that's appropriate. The house charm opens to reveal two little hearts, which is all that would fit, and for Anne that's all it takes to make her house a home.

Anne's Bracelet

COFFEEPOT

When it comes to coffee, plain old "good to the last drop" is Anne's favorite. Add milk and sugar, that's fine. But don't whip it, froth it, or flavor it. She's likely to get ugly if you do because you're messing with a ritual she uses to make her feel more at home in strange places. Anne counts on coffee to show its familiar face in remote places of the world where the familiar isn't easy to find. It's been the one friend to greet her in every country she's called home. Each time she steps off a plane her nose searches until it finds it. When the aroma reaches her it gently reassures her she's right where she ought to be. She prepares her cup the same way each time, one cube of sugar and a splash of milk. Then she sits and slowly sips for a few minutes to get her bearings and think of the next right thing to do. In a world of so much travel and relocation, it's good to have a familiar anchor you can count on. For Anne it's just a cup of coffee, for me it's putting on a favorite sweater, for a friend it's putting up pictures. But in each case these rituals can help us feel, as Anne puts it, "like I've come home to a place I've never been before."

63

Anne's Bracelet

WATERING CAN

While living in Passos, Brazil, my sister was determined to grow her own garden. The fruit and vegetables she found in the local marketplace weren't very tasty, and she needed a project to occupy her time and keep her two-year-old son, Liam, entertained. But the surrounding forest and the animals that lived there took a different view of Anne's efforts. Their personal takeout restaurant had arrived. They scampered, flew, crawled, and galloped from miles away to get their share. Anne tried everything from aluminum pie plates to lights to keep them away. A few months into the frustration of trying to protect her plot, she notice that Liam started to go to the window every day at dusk to wait for the "aminals" to appear. She realized that the garden provided him with his first look at real rabbits, foxes, deer, and birds. Sitting with Liam at the window each night talking about the animals they watched in the garden was the real harvest she was meant to reap.

TOILET

Anne's son Liam was a pretty good student in potty training. He learned all the words to "On Top of the Potty" (sung to the tune of "On Top of Old Smoky"), he overcame his fear of being plucked down into the toilet bowl by monsters, and he even learned to make regular trips to the bathroom just in case. But the real stumper was "Where does it go when I flush the toilet?" Liam was skeptical of the septic system story, so Anne finally told him that after we sit on the potty it all goes to "potty heaven." One day Anne found Liam sitting on the toilet in deep concentration. "What are you doing, Liam?" she asked. He looked up from his efforts and whispered, "Shhhhh, Mommy, I'm making angels." The logic of an explanation is always acknowledged by the logic of the response.

Anne's Bracelet

SANTA BOOT

One Christmas Eve Anne's daughter, Dylan, decided that Santa needed some extra help in order to deliver presents properly. So she got Anne's bracelet out of her jewelry box and took this charm between two fingers. Carefully she pried open the top of the little boot and Santa popped out. Looking him straight in his little coal-black eye, Dylan gave him these last-minute instructions: 1. Make sure you know I'm at *this* house. 2. Get cats to pull the sleigh, not "waim deers." Cats are jumpier. 3. Eat the cookie and milk we left you. 4. Don't make a big mess 'cause Mommy will be mad. At the end of the input session Dylan pushed Santa down, shut the lid, laughed, and said, "Bye, Santa, see ya soon." As she watched Dylan trot away, Anne remembered what our mother once told her: "When life seems a little dull, spend fifteen minutes with a four-year-old. She'll take you on a trip to the improbable, where the impossible can happen and the unbelievable always comes true."

A real dollar bill is folded inside this charm, which comes with directions etched on the side, "In emergency, break glass," and its own little hammer to do the job. My sister shares the dirty family secret: she loves scratch-off lottery tickets. Anytime she has a lonely dollar bill lying around, she sneaks off to the local 7-Eleven for her fix. The odds stink, the games are dumb, and all she gets most of the time is a mess of silver shavings, but it's the possibility that makes it fun and keeps her scratching. I hope she never has to open up the charm to get this dollar, but if she does, she's in good company. Throughout history, great things have happened because men and women were willing to take chances. Certainly Anne buying a Lotto ticket doesn't compare to Ben Franklin flying his kite, but they share the spirit of "maybe this time." As Anne has said before, "Taking the next chance is sometimes the bridge between you and your jackpot."

DEVIL IN THE SHAKER

Anne has a practical view about everything, especially when it comes to life issues. She believes that people struggling with addictions are not completely powerless. They may be powerless *after* taking that drink or using that drug or indulging in any unhealthy behavior, but they have a choice in their actions. All they have to do is shout, "No, not today!" and stop for that moment. Right then they have made the first step to freedom. Yes, the road will be rough along the way to recovery. But Anne always reminds me, "When you chase away your inner demons you'll find the angels at your feet."

Anne's Bracelet

ABACUS

The abacus is a defiant little charm that breaks all the rules of the charm-collecting game; it has no special meaning for its owner, it's not an item people use in daily life, and it isn't a rare piece. It's just a fun, oddball charm and another example of Anne's penchant for surprising the family at the strangest moments.

Anne got married on a beautiful September day. A few hours into the reception she and her new husband, along with most of the wedding party, headed out for a walk on the beach down the block. Suddenly Anne peeled off her wedding gown and made a beeline for the ocean to take a postnuptial dip. I noticed what appeared to be a piece of confetti stuck to her rear end. It was a tattoo. But it wasn't the typical flower, bird, or heart. It was a tattoo of Winnie-the-Pooh, about the size of a quarter, with the "huney" jar stuck on his head. Before she left that night I asked her what possessed her to put a bear on her butt. "Hey," she said, "I don't want to waste my time on the predictable. I want to count every moment and make every moment count in my own special way."

MAXINE'S

BRACELET

Maxine's father wasn't big on public shows of affection, so my aunt grew up believing that she was a disappointment to him. She felt like a piece of furniture that didn't quite fit with the decor her father had in mind. It wasn't until his sudden death in 1972 that she came to know how wrong her assessment had been. After her father died Max visited his office for the first time in twenty-two years, and she was unprepared for what she found. Behind his desk was a credenza filled with pictures of her, the wood surface barely visible. She was leaning over the fence at the monkey house, eating cake at her tenth birthday party, accepting her high school diploma, twirling at a dance recital, lying in her mother's arms just hours old, posing on her wedding day, giving a bath to her own daughter. There were forty-two frames of every size and shape. On the back wall of Max's bedroom is a picture of her father surrounded by the many photographs of her she found that day. Alongside the arrangement is a little framed note: "The True Picture of Love Is Often What Your Eyes Never See."

Maxine's Bracelet

Max always volunteers at elementary schools, helping to bring the arts to young children. She chaperones field trips, invites artists and musicians into the classroom, and finds ways to provide instruments and art supplies for the children to explore their own talents. One year she made a series of weekly visits to a third grade class to teach the children different forms of painting. Each child was asked to paint a picture that would be entered in an art competition the final week of Max's visits. When the time came, disaster struck. Minutes before the pictures were put up for display, an open can of paint spilled all over the painting belonging to Edward, a shy, unpopular boy who sat in the back of the class. He was devastated, but with no time to paint another he had to put his damaged picture up with the others. One of Max's artist friends volunteered to be the judge for art competition, and to everyone's surprise, Edward won first place. "The children had their first lesson in the complexities of art that day," Max told me. "Sometimes when curiosity connects with catastrophe at just the right moment, a masterpiece is born."

ELF

With Max, every day brings a startling bit of information. We were at the store looking at shoes one day when she picked up a pair of belled slippers and announced, "Clowns scare the hell out of me." I stared at her. She went on, "Everyone else sees a jolly imp; I see a violent, disfigured person with a big nose, wearing my old Aunt May's makeup, who wants to stuff me in his little car." Max told me her parents used to take her to the circus every year, and every year she'd cry at the sight of clowns. But to their surprise, she wanted to go back every time the circus came through town. She couldn't bear to miss the acrobats and lions.

"Sometimes," Max said, "you gotta deal with the clowns in life if you want to enjoy the rest of the day."

Maxine's Bracelet

In her early twenties, Max joined the Peace Corps. She went down to South America to assist families in remote villages where children routinely  died from dehydration, anemia, bacterial infections, and other afflictions. By working with the local doctors, she hoped to learn enough to better the lives of the people she met. But on her first day she was dismayed to watch a university-trained doctor delay treatment of a critically ill child by telling the young mother she was to wait and give the medicine he prescribed for her baby on the first day of the full moon. Alarmed, Max intervened. The doctor yelled at her furiously.

After things calmed down a bit, the doctor quietly explained to her that as a doctor of Western medicine he had to be sensitive to traditional medicines if he wanted to get local people to visit him at all. If he shunned their culture they would in turn shun him, and many other children would die needlessly. Max worked with many other fine doctors during her stay and came to realize that as a nurse her role was to listen to patients as well as treat them. "I'll tell you something, my dear," Max said over a glass of iced tea one afternoon. "The day you think you know it all is the day you find out you don't understand a thing."

75

Max is one of those people who carry a complete pharmacy around in their purse. Safety pins, bandages, alcohol swabs, tissue, vitamins, panty hose, tampons, hand lotion, and an astounding assortment of breath mints can be found in her cavernous bag. At the mall one day with Max, after battling strollers and slow-moving shoppers, I developed a powerful headache. Max had taken her wallet from her bag and left to get a soda. I pulled the bag over and began pawing through the contents in search of aspirin. I immediately found a pickle jar–sized bottle that took both hands to get out of the bag. "I always have lots of aspirin on hand," she remarked when she rejoined me, "but they're just props. When I offer someone an aspirin I'm really offering my concern. And that usually leads to a conversation that both of us benefit from. The other person feels cared for and I feel needed, all because of two little tablets."

Maxine's Bracelet

TELEPHONE

I was complaining to Max one day about Sheila from work, who was calling me at all hours to whine about her boyfriend.

I told Max that if it was past eleven at night and the phone rang, it was always Sheila on the other end. She'd tell me all about the latest problem: "He's never on time, he never calls, he must be cheating on me, he has an illegitimate child I just found out about," blah, blah, blah. It's all I ever heard from this wacko.

Max, who never sugarcoated what she had to say, put down her coffee cup, folded her hands under her chin, and after a pause said, "Hey, sweetie pie, next time that weird woman from the office calls you after eleven to talk about her problems, don't get off the phone too fast. One day *you* might be that weird woman from the office with lots of problems who needs a friend to talk to. Let's hope that when the time comes, you get through to someone who has a little more patience."

COCKTAIL GLASSES

Max is a master entertainer who can work a room like no one else. Her connections to the world of the rich and powerful are legendary, so her announcement in the late 1980s that she was opening a posh restaurant in Washington, D.C., was big news. Every politician, CEO, and actor who had ever been to one of her infamous house parties was after an invitation to her opening night. Her tables booked faster than seats at Belmont to watch Secretariat run a back-from-the-grave mile and a half. And she didn't disappoint. The night was a smashing success. I asked Max to tell me the secret to being a great hostess. She smiled. "Honey, be it castle or cabin, celebrities or salesmen, there are three rules for great entertaining: make every person the center of attention, prepare every plate like it was being served to the fussiest restaurant critic, and never let anyone leave without a warm embrace and an invitation to drop by anytime."

Maxine's Bracelet

CASH REGISTER

Many years ago, at the end of a busy night at her restaurant, Max poked her head into the kitchen. She startled a newly hired dishwasher, Jazz, as he wrapped up a small sirloin and stashed it in his pack. Jazz looked at her and, without a word, walked out the back door into the alley. Furious, Max ran outside after him. But she paused when she saw him talking to a small figure huddled against the Dumpster. It was one of the homeless women who camped in an abandoned house on the next block with her two young children. Max watched as Jazz handed the package to the woman, gave her a gentle pat on the shoulder, and continued on his way. Max turned and slipped back inside the restaurant. Max and Jazz have never spoken about that night. But every Friday around eleven, they share a ritual in the back kitchen. Jazz wraps up a small steak and puts it in his pack. Max, leaning against the doorway with her arms crossed, watches him walk out and locks the door behind him. It's a reminder to her that it's not the amount of cash in the register that counts, it's the amount of change in your heart.

Maxine's Bracelet

In the high-end restaurant Max runs, the window of time that defines outstanding service is narrow and sensitive. Customers sitting at the same table expect that all their plates will arrive together and at the correct serving temperatures for each dish. A sixty-to-ninety-second wait for a lagging meal can turn a rave review into a tepid mention. It takes only a few of these timing blunders, especially at the table of an undercover critic, to blow the coveted "best of" title, so Max makes sure that time is on the minds of all of her employees. Right inside the door to the kitchen, up on a shelf at eye level, Max has an old-fashioned hourglass. It stands one foot tall, making it impossible to miss. She makes frequent stops during the night to turn over the glass so the sands are always running. Every waiter, chef, assistant, hostess, and busboy sees it on his or her rounds. The large bronze plate above the glass reminds them minute by minute that "time well valued is always time well spent."

Las Vegas is the pinnacle of people watching, making it one of Max's favorite vacation spots. A bank of slot machines is to Max what the jungle watering hole is to a wildlife photographer. One evening, staked out at her favorite casino, Max spied an elderly woman sitting at three slot machines tucked away in a quiet corner. Her clothes were tattered, and it looked like all she owned was stuffed in the four shopping bags piled at her feet.

She was feeding coins to each machine in turn with the care of a mother bird feeding her chicks. She played the machines in the same order every time— one, two, three, and then back to one. Max struck up a conversation with her and commented on all the quarters sitting in the trays of the three slot machines. The little woman looked up at Max and wheezed, "Remember, dear, if you work hard enough your luck will never run out."

Maxine's Bracelet

Max's great-uncle Macky was a nasty hermit. He lived with a snappy terrier in a little shack at the end of a scruffy street. He was so mean even the stray cats in the neighborhood skipped his house on their door-to-door mooching trips. Macky kept all of his money—which was rumored to be a considerable sum—in a small black safe under the floorboards of his kitchen. When he died suddenly of a heart attack at the age of ninety-two, Max knew that her ship had come in, and she knew it was a very big ship. As Macky's only living heir, Max inherited the house, the churlish dog, and the locked safe. The safe was so heavy that a flatbed truck with a winch and three men were needed to bring it to her house. One of the last locksmiths to take a crack at opening the safe finally fingered the dial to the right numbers. Max's fortune-hunting heart was beating a mile a minute as the door opened. The only thing inside the safe was an envelope. The only thing inside the envelope was a three-by-five card. The only thing on the three-by-five card was the combination to the safe. "My uncle Macky didn't leave me much," Max complained, "but he did leave me with one last lesson: expectation unbounded always leads to disappointment compounded."

Maxine's Bracelet

Max married once for love and once for money. Her first husband—big, brash, and handsome—ran off with the local dog trainer. The second husband—old, rich, and childish—died of a heart attack while he was fishing off the coast of South America. Max admits that she made some wrong choices when it came to her own marriages, but that's what makes her so helpful to other wedding hopefuls who find themselves trapped in the premarital tar pit known as dating. During my own tar pit days, Max shook her finger at me and explained that my poor choice in men was directly connected to my low self-esteem. In a scolding tone she told me that we get the partner we feel we deserve. I realized that the reason I was dating thoughtless men was because I felt unworthy to accept thoughtfulness. And as Max predicted, once I finally fixed myself, the right man did indeed find his way into my life, and I emerged triumphant from the pit. Max said it all one day when she explained, "Sit in the mud and the pigs will find you. Put yourself in the palace and the prince will prevail."

Maxine's Bracelet

Max had been a scriptwriter for a popular soap opera. She wrote lines for Julie, a virginal young nurse who kept getting into car accidents. But with all of the time Julie spent in head bandages, coming up with memorable scenes proved to be a problem. Max decided to get herself, and Julie, out of the predicament by creating Julie's evil twin sister, Joan. Her boss loved it. The show's sponsor loved the new character too. With her monstrous scheming, Joan proved to be worth her weight in laundry detergent. Ratings skyrocketed. Unfortunately, Max didn't get the credit for creating Joan. Her boss, a monstrous schemer himself, presented the idea as his own and took all of the kudos instead. While soap opera historians never credited Max for the creation of one of the most beloved daytime villainesses in history, Max says it's never bothered her. "The only person I ever try to impress with my talent is me. When someone else takes credit for my work I just take it as a sign that I'm a lot better than I thought."

Max's art is her sewing. Her friends have admired her outfits for years, often begging her to recreate them. Huge brightly flowing caftans,

slipper flats, and big, chunky Bakelite jewelry of all descriptions make up her trademark look, along with a tasteful turban to complete the outfit. Max is so good because she's been sewing since college. While most of the other young women were making daisy chains and learning the guitar chords to the latest protest song, Max was zipping out a new creation with her Singer. Max would rather create than complain. But Max's sewing has meaning beyond creating the next new outfit. She uses endless sewing analogies to impart her wisdom. One of my favorites is about life: "Use the unique fabric of talent God gave you, the patterns of right and wrong your parents taught you, and then thread them together with persistence and optimism and you'll find that you'll wear pretty well in life."

LIPSTICK

Max, with her flair for color and fashion, has always been a pro at applying makeup. Young women who worked for her routinely flocked to her for advice, and Max uses great care in instructing them. By far her most lengthy lessons are on selecting and applying lipstick. Max insists on a few lipstick rules for life.

Find one shade and stick with it. Never go out in public without it on. Check your teeth regularly for smudges. Reapply at regular intervals during the day—discreetly. But above all, she emphasizes that wearing lipstick carries with it responsibilities and consequences. "Remember, girls, lipstick leaves your lips behind. So drink, blot, and kiss with care, because you never know who'll find the evidence."

One day I was fiddling with all of the cosmetics on Max's makeup table in her bedroom. Among her creams, lotions, toners, and foundations was a bottle of the perfume Max has worn since I've known her, a spicy, full-bodied scent that hovers in the air without overpowering everything around it. It creates an aura around Max that both women and men are drawn to, like cats to a sun-drenched porch. I picked up the bottle and commented to Max how much I liked the scent on her. As she put away a few pairs of stockings she had washed she told me that when she was between jobs in her early twenties she worked at the perfume counter in Saks Fifth Avenue for a few months. The older, more experienced women behind the counters taught her to tell the difference between a cheap scent and an expensive one by using her sense of smell alone. "I got the nose test down," she said, "but the technical stuff those perfume guerrillas tried to teach me went way over my head. All I ever figured out in the end was that a well-blended perfume is like a favorite dinner guest. It never disrupts the room when it arrives, and it never lingers too long at the end of the evening."

"Forget about how-to books, pundits, and experts. If you have a problem, take a nature walk." This sounded pretty strange coming from a woman whose idea of experiencing the great outdoors was doing her nails by the pool. But being in a tough spot at the time, I listened to Max anyway. One day many years ago, Max said, she was sitting on her sofa, exhausted after another unsuccessful search for her car keys. She was late for work again, with no other place to look. She glanced out the window and noticed a squirrel zipping around, burying acorns one after the other. Within a few minutes he had buried fifteen to twenty nuts near his tree. At that rate, she figured that in a month or two the squirrel would have planted so many nuts he'd have no problem finding one to eat in the dead of winter, even if he forgot most of the hiding spots. After she finished her story, Max took me around her house and showed me place after place where she had stashed duplicate sets of keys. She paused and gestured to the woods beyond. "Pay close attention to Mother Nature," she said. "She'll give you a good kick in the pants every once in a while just to remind you that you're only human."

Maxine's Bracelet

Max plans her day around the Weather Channel. If it looks like rain, she usually curtails her errands to avoid the traffic backups that result. If the day looks sunny, she may stop by the nursery to pick up some petunias she's been wanting to plant. But as accurate as forecasters are these days, there's always a chance the weather will take an unexpected turn. When this happens Max calmly alters her plans, changes her clothes, and adapts as best she can. When cancer struck, she behaved no differently. Max immediately assessed her situation. "There's a storm in my body that's quickly building strength. Its path is unclear, and it could change at any time, so I've got all of my emergency plans ready—chemo treatments, a good diet, great friends, and time for prayer. Like a boarded-up house, I'll ride this one out for better or worse."

After she was free of the cancer, Max often impressed upon me that I won't ever be able to control change; I can only keep change from controlling me. After preparing as best I can, all that is left to do is look to the horizon, smile, and greet the day.

AFTERWORD

Charm collecting is a great way to pass family history and hobbies from one generation to the next. Regardless of the size of your pocketbook or the aim of your collecting, you can find a category of charms just for you. ¶My interest in collecting came from growing up with the bracelets worn by my mother and grandmother. My grandmother, Elsie, and my mother, Pat, collected the charms on their bracelets over a thirty-year period, starting in 1940. The charms on my sister Anne and aunt Maxine's bracelets are ones I collected during the eighties and nineties. The charms featured on all of the bracelets are heavy, three-dimensional pieces crafted by goldsmiths during the thirties, forties, fifties, and sixties. Many are rare "mechanicals," charms with intricate moving parts. In the past, these mechanicals were readily available in jewelry stores and gift shops. Today, because of the high cost of creating these types of charms, most can be found only in antique stores, estate sales, and auction houses. ¶The eBay auction site, with its accessibility and competitive pricing atmosphere, has opened up charm collecting to a much larger audience. Well-crafted gold mechanical charms sell here for anywhere between fifty and two hundred dollars each. For people looking for a less expensive alternative, silver mechanicals are also

Charm Collecting

available and tend to sell for between ten and seventy-five dollars. And for the more frugal collector, both plated gold and silver flat charms can be purchased at a significantly lower cost, allowing a collector to put together a ten-charm silver bracelet for as little as thirty dollars. ¶The types of charms are endless. Some collectors choose themes such as gardening, sports, animals, travel, and hobbies. Others collect charms that broadly define the history of their lives, celebrating events such as the birth of a child, date of graduation, favorite travel destinations, and anniversaries. Still other collectors, like me, focus on charms simply because of their unique nature. My collection includes a little Bible with real pages, a card-deck charm with fifty-two real cards, a glass case that contains a miniature pair of glasses, and a money charm with a real dollar bill inside. ¶If collecting seems a long or intimidating process, many already-completed gold and silver charm bracelets are available at every price level. Simple silver charm bracelets are found in a number of catalogs and stores for as little as twenty-five dollars. More elaborate estate bracelets range from five hundred to five thousand dollars and can be found on eBay and through estate jewelry stores. ¶Few books are available on charm collecting or the history of charms. *Charms to Collect,* by Marjorie Congram (Dockwra Press, 1998), is by far the best

AFTERWORD

I've found. It's a lovely little book that gives some history and has lots of pictures of unusual pieces. It can be special ordered through your local or on-line bookseller. ¶ Charm collecting is a wonderful way to record family history. The bracelets become golden scrapbooks that are proudly worn around the wrists of each new generation. Long after the original owner is gone, her story remains fresh and new, becoming more poignant as the years pass. Whatever your passion or purpose in collecting charms, I wish you the best of luck and the most cherished of memories.

Kathleen Oldford, April 2001

CHARMOLOGY

I have tried to provide information about each charm, but sadly, details on some of them remain a mystery. If a charm comes from my personal collection I have provided comments on how I came to find it and/or a description of any unique features I think would interest the reader. And here is some history on this unusual art form, which might also be of interest. ❡Mechanicals, charms with moving parts, gained popularity after World War II. Returning soldiers would pick up simple keepsake charms for their sweethearts on the journey home. Seeing the popularity of these charms, jewelers and goldsmiths in America took charm jewelry one step further by adding moving parts, jewels, and enamel. By the 1950s, women of all ages were sporting charm bracelets on their wrists bulging with charms given by parents, friends, and beaux. ❡As the price of gold skyrocketed in the early 1970s, the more elaborate mechanical charms began to disappear from jewelry stores. But happily, an active collector market for these charms has emerged introducing the world of charms to a new generation.

CHARMOLOGY

CHARMOLOGY

Charms can be found almost anywhere. Here a few charm-rich resources to plumb:

STORES WITH NATIONAL LOCATIONS

Service Merchandise
1-888-764-4387
www.servicemerchandise.com

Zales
1-800-311-5393
www.zales.com

Kay Jewelers
1-800-877-8169
www.kay.com

ON-LINE RESOURCES

www.ebay.com
www.charmworks.com
www.the-way-we-were.com
www.rembrandtcharms.com

ALSO, VISIT

www.mymotherscharms.com, the most comprehensive charm and charm bracelet collecting community site on the Internet.